Estate
Planning

By Marc Robinson

 TIME LIFE BOOKS ®

Alexandria, Virginia

State Street Global Advisors: educating people about money
For 200 years, we have been in the banking business helping people manage and invest their money. We are a global leader in the investment management industry, serving institutions and individuals worldwide.

Our goal in creating this series is to give you unbiased, useful information that will help you manage your money. No product advertisements. No sales pitches. Just straightforward, understandable information.

Our ultimate hope is that after reading these books you feel more informed, more in control of your money, and perhaps most importantly, more able to successfully plan and reach your financial goals.

Time-Life Books is a division of
TIME LIFE INCORPORATED

Time-Life Custom Publishing
Vice President and Publisher: Terry Newell
Director of Sales: Neil Levin
Director, New Business Development: Phyllis A. Gardner
Senior Art Director: Christopher M. Register
Managing Editor: Donia Ann Steele
Production Manager: Carolyn Bounds
Quality Assurance Manager: James D. King

© 1996 Top Down

Books produced by Time-Life Custom Publishing are available at special bulk discount for promotional and premium use. Custom adaptations can also be created to meet your specific marketing goals.
Call 1-800-323-5255

For State Street Global Advisors,
The Lab:
Clark Kellogg
Jenny Phillips
Sally Nellson
Paul Schwartz
For Top Down:
Marc Robinson
Mark Shepherd
Design: Adams/Morioka, Inc.

Robinson, Marc, 1955-
    Estate planning / by Marc Robinson.
       p.   cm. – (Time Life Books your money matters)
    ISBN 0-7835-4811-7
    1. Estate planning–United States–Popular works.
I. Title. II. Series.
KF750.Z9R584 1996
346.7305′2–dc20   96-3237
[347.30652]   CIP

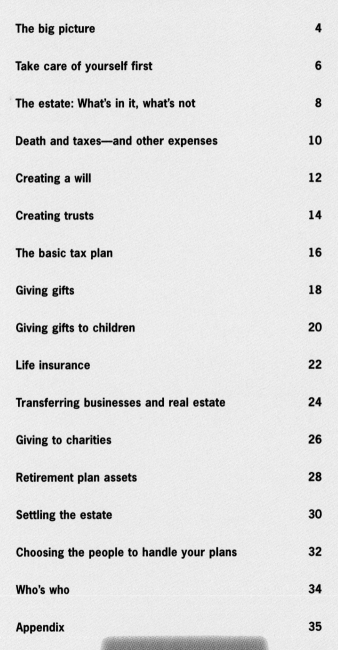

TABLE OF Contents

The big picture

If you own property, you have an estate—and some decisions to make. How will you take care of yourself and your loved ones? How will you find ways to save money, provide for your well-being, minimize taxes? How will you maximize your lifestyle while you're alive, then maximize what your family and friends receive when you're gone? These aren't just questions for the rich. Everyone's life is the same puzzle. And every decision is up to you:

How will you organize and simplify the rest of your life—
not just your death?

Protect yourself while you're alive

Someday, you may become incapacitated and be unable to care for yourself. Fortunately, you can use simple, legally permissible documents, such as a power of attorney and a living will, to write instructions on taking care of your health and your wealth, and to name someone you trust to act as your surrogate.

Manage your assets while you're alive

You can use estate planning strategies, particularly trusts, to help you:

- minimize taxes;
- shield assets from potential (not existing) creditors;
- protect your financial privacy;
- maximize the use of your assets;
- increase your income;
- manage finances for those who can't (or shouldn't) do it themselves;
- give family and friends some financial, educational, and medical support;
- appoint someone to help manage your assets—from providing assistance to handling everything.

{ **Keep in mind: This is general information**
This book provides only general information about estate planning. Every person's situation is unique. State laws differ, as well. It's best to get professional legal and tax advice when planning your estate.

{ **Be aware of split ownership.** If you want to give someone an asset you own jointly, you'll need the other owner to sign as well. When you die, anything you own jointly goes to the other owner, no matter what your intention. (A common tax-planning strategy among spouses is to divide the assets and own them separately.)

Direct distribution of assets after you're gone

There are many strategies, including trusts and a will, you can use to:

- decide who will get what and when (assets don't have to go to others immediately after you die);
- try to provide enough cash to cover the expenses of dying (e.g., funeral, debts, taxes);
- control what can and can't be done with your property;
- appoint one or more people to manage the assets on your behalf;
- appoint someone to settle all the affairs of your estate;
- appoint a guardian to care for underage children.

Governments are waiting for your money
Your home state may be able to tax your personal assets. Any state in which you own real estate may be able to tax the property value. The federal government may be able to tax anything, no matter where it is. If you try to give away too much to avoid taxes, you could be taxed on that, too.

People can help you
There's a lot to do to prepare your estate: for example, deciding who you will choose to manage any trusts, follow instructions in your will, and care for loved ones if you can't. Then there's tax planning, investment management, and all the legalities. What should you do yourself and what should you delegate? Who should help—a friend, a relative, a professional?

Take care of yourself firs

Someday, you may be unable to make your own medical or financial decisions. But you can prearrange for someone to be there to make decision according to your wishes. Three simple, legally binding documents let you name that important person (or people) and give specific instructions and general guidance. You can help ensure that your wishes are respected and affairs kept in order,

by setting up these safety nets.

Protect your health

Healthcare power of attorney

This document must be signed by you and notarized. Use it to authorize someone you trust to make medical decisions for you if you can't, and to provide guidelines for making day-to-day medical decisions.

Some examples include:

- taking certain medicines;
- performing surgery or chemotherapy;
- at-home or nursing home care.

Protect your dignity

The living will

This document lets you create a list of circumstances in which you would refuse life-sustaining treatment. For example, you may not want to be kept alive artificially if there is no hope for recovery. Some states require you to sign a living will in front of witnesses.

{ **If you live in more than one state.** Since these documents are usually needed in an emergency, make sure all your doctors in each state have a copy of your healthcare power of attorney and your living will.

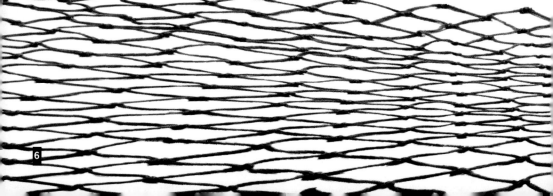

Check-box forms. Some states have state-approved forms you can buy that allow you to check boxes based on your wishes. Of course you can always make your own custom versions instead.

Communicate! Medical and financial decisions must often be made quickly when you're seriously ill. Talk extensively with the people you've authorized so they clearly understand your wishes. Consider choosing people who live relatively close and who can manage the affairs reasonably. Give copies to each person and to your doctors.

Protect your wealth

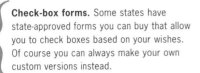

The durable power of attorney

This document authorizes the one you name (the "attorney-in-fact") to handle all your financial affairs if you're unable to do so. It's a useful document to be sure your real estate will be managed, your investments handled, and your bills paid. You can make the powers effective upon signing or only if you become incapacitated.

You can create a "general" power that permits the person to handle virtually anything, or a "limited" power that authorizes only specific functions.

Without a durable power of attorney, your finances may become a matter for the courts to handle. The court will appoint a "conservator" to manage your finances, and the proceedings will be of public record.

States are different. Not all states recognize a living will, which doesn't mean you can't have one. The document can serve as guidance; it just won't be legally enforceable.

The estate:
What's in it, what's not

Anything and everything you have is part of your estate. A major goal of estate planning is to reduce your taxable estate even as you accumulate assets, so that you pay as little as possible in estate taxes. Having an idea of your estate's value while you're alive, therefore, can help you plan properly for taking care of yourself and those you care about. Particularly when you include the value of your home, life insurance, and retirement plan,

you may be **worth more** than you think.

What's in

- All assets owned in your name: cash, securities, cars, real estate, personal property, and so on.
- The full value of life insurance (the full death benefit, not merely the cash value).
- Money you're owed.
- Any jointly held property.
- A business.
- Anything not in your name but which you control.

What's not

Any asset you've given away permanently and completely. (You've kept no control and receive no benefits from it.)

Debts. Money owed to creditors reduces the value of your estate.

Gifts to a spouse. Unlimited assets can be passed between spouses free from gift and estate taxes, as long as the recipient is a U.S. citizen. It's called the "marital deduction." Actually, it's a deferral. Any assets that avoid an estate tax when you die may be taxed when your spouse dies.

Gifts to others. You may make a gift of cash or property. It isn't taxable as income to the recipient and it's out of your estate.

In or out? Some assets transferred within three years of your death will be re-included in your estate when calculating taxes.

Whom can you give to? Anyone or any organization can be the recipient (a "beneficiary") of your assets. Be as specific as possible in naming them in a will, trust, or insurance policy to avoid confusion and conflicts. Generally gifts to pets aren't enforceable. If you want to do it anyway, consult a lawyer.

It ends with probate. Probate is the court-run process of distributing your assets after you die. Making transfers before you die can save money and time, and assure that property goes to those you want to receive it.

Upon death...

$0

Trusts. Any asset you transfer into an "irrevocable" trust (one you can't alter) is out of your estate, as long as you aren't a beneficiary of the trust. Assets placed into revocable trusts remain in your estate because you've reserved the right to take them back. Generally, if you move an asset out of your estate but continue to receive income earned from it, the asset will come back into your estate upon your death.

The will. When you die, assets held in your name alone—the "rest and residue"—of your estate are distributed according to your instructions. This doesn't include any assets owned jointly or that are already payable directly to a beneficiary.

   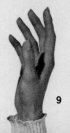

Death and taxes—
and other expenses

Generally, assets you don't own, control, or have an interest in when you die are out of your estate and not taxable. But if an asset is in your estate, the federal and state governments will want some of it. If you try to transfer an asset, they may tax that, too. Fortunately, there are plenty of opportunities to avoid paying taxes. Still, when it comes to determining what's taxable and then calculating the taxes owed,

many people **underestimate** their estate's tax liability.

Taxes on transfers

Gift tax. The IRS may tax transfers of assets you make while alive (see the next column, "What's tax-free").

Federal estate tax. The government looks at the value of the assets left in your estate and taxes it before it's distributed. Rates are higher than income tax rates: The lowest bracket is 37%; the highest is 55%.

State taxes. Some states have a "sponge tax," which means they simply claim a portion of the federal tax paid. Other states have an inheritance tax or their own estate tax.

Generation-skipping tax. An extra tax of 55% applies to transfers to grandchildren (and some others, according to a complicated set of rules).

Foreign taxes. There may be additional taxes if there are assets or beneficiaries in other countries.

What's tax-free

Tax laws let you transfer assets without being taxed until you reach a certain value threshold. Here are some examples.

Marital deduction. Unlimited amounts can be transferred between spouses while they're alive or upon death—if the recipient is a U.S. citizen.

Annual gift tax exclusion. It may be the best tool for transfers while you're alive. Every person can give up to $10,000 a year per recipient (no limit on the number). To qualify, the recipient must have "immediate use and enjoyment" of the asset.

Unified credit. Up to $600,000 of assets goes untaxed when transferred. You and your spouse each get this credit—but you must each have the assets *in your own names* (not shared). So, while alive or upon death, a married couple can transfer up to $1.2 million without paying gift or estate taxes.

Generation-skipping exemption. Up to $1 million of assets (per person) can be transferred free from the 55% generation-skipping tax.

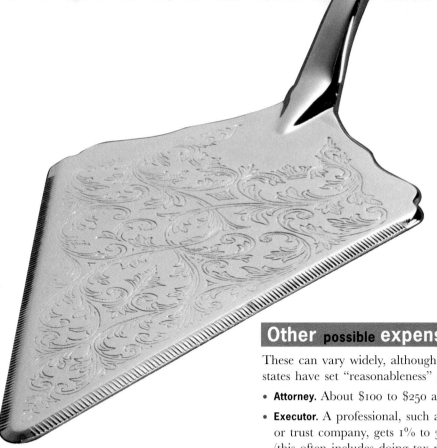

Other possible expenses

These can vary widely, although many states have set "reasonableness" guidelines.

- **Attorney.** About $100 to $250 an hour.
- **Executor.** A professional, such as a bank or trust company, gets 1% to 3% of assets (this often includes doing tax returns, managing assets, and so on).
- **Appraiser.** Someone to place a credible value on the assets gets an hourly fee.
- **Accountant.** A flat fee or hourly rate for preparing tax returns.
- **Storage, shipping.** For furniture or other personal property.
- **Court filing fees.** Typically under $500.
- **Funeral expenses.** Usually $1,000 to $5,000.
- **Debts.** The recipient of an asset becomes responsible for paying any debts on the asset (e.g., car payments). Any debts not tied to an asset are paid by the estate.

Taxes on income

The trust's income tax. Dividend and interest income earned by a trust could be taxable to you, the trust, or the beneficiary. (Irrevocable trusts reach the high tax brackets sooner than individuals. For example, in 1996, any income over $7,900 was taxed at 39.6%.)

The estate's income tax. A tax on the income earned by the estate while it was being settled.

Other income tax. A tax the beneficiaries must pay on earnings and distributions from assets such as retirement plans and annuities. To many, this comes as a surprise.

{ **Creditors first.** Any outstanding debts are paid from the estate before assets are distributed. The money for that may come from:

| • life insurance | • cash in the estate | • selling assets | • payments from a trust |

Creating a will

The purpose of a will is to: pass on assets that haven't already been distributed through a trust or by gift; express any limits on the use of your assets; name the person (the executor) who will manage the final affairs; and name a guardian for any underage children. It's a crucial document, because if you die without a will (die "intestate"), state law will decide who gets what, who handles everything, and who cares for your children. In other words, your will is the place

to collect your remaining thoughts and possessions.

Give directions

Be clear and give positive directions, because any ambiguities will be resolved based on your supposed "intent." The three key purposes of a will are to:

- specify what should go to whom, when, and under what conditions;
- name a guardian for underage or incapacitated children;
- name an executor to carry out your wishes.

Bring the right people

Each state has its own formalities. In general, you must be at least 18 and of sound mind when you write your will. Most states require two or three people to witness your signature. (A witness shouldn't be someone who's receiving something in your will.) The will should be "notarized"—an assurance that you and the witnesses are signing freely, appear to be competent, and are whom you say you are. In some states, this speeds up the process.

What can go in it

Anything—whether of sentimental or monetary value.

Solely owned assets. A will is useless for a jointly owned asset or one that is already payable directly to a beneficiary, such as life insurance and retirement plans. Those assets will automatically go to the joint owner or beneficiary, no matter what the will says.

Separated personals. Experts recommend creating a separate provision to give away personal property. If you don't, some could be sold to cover expenses instead of going to your heirs.

Controlling from the grave. You can require people to do certain things before receiving an asset—but not just anything. For instance, you can't insist on a child marrying a particular person, or someone converting to a religion. These kinds of restrictions go against public policy.

Where to keep it. Somewhere easily located. Give it to your lawyer or another professional, or keep it in a "personals" drawer at home.

{ **Maintaining privacy.** Since a will is of public record, some people attach a separate memo that won't be made public and spells out any intentions or special directions for your executor to follow. You can also include last wishes that won't be binding but could still be carried out by the executor.

Who can get it

You can name anyone to receive whatever you want. It's also important to name "contingent beneficiaries." These are the people you want to receive assets if the first beneficiaries can't.

Kinds of legacies. A legacy is what you leave behind for others. There are four kinds:

- specifically named property
- general gifts of money
- gifts of money from specific sources
- gifts of whatever remains after all expenses have been paid.

Anyone can contest. To contest a will, your heirs can file an objection with the probate court. There is a legal presumption that children weren't meant to be cut out, unless the language is clear. Generally, states don't permit spouses to be cut out entirely.

hanging your mind

ɔu can:

write a new will that clearly revokes the old one;

write a codicil (the fancy name for an amendment) if you're making minor changes;

revoke it entirely by tearing it up or burning it (preferably in front of others).

When to re-do the will

Certain life events should trigger a new look: marriage, death of a spouse, divorce, a birth, remarriage, moving to a new state.

Creating trusts

You can think of a trust like an account: You arrange for someone—the trustee—to hold and manage any assets you contribute to the trust, and to provide for the benefit of others, called "beneficiaries." You can create a trust to do almost anything—including taking care of yourself in times of severe illness. Different goals call for different kinds of trusts, but for people who don't want to totally give up control or use of an asset,

the most common is a revocable, living trust.

You open it

With a revocable trust, you may change the terms or end it at any time. Basically, with this trust, you:

- name yourself, someone close to you, or a professional as trustee to manage the assets and handle distributions (it's also wise to name a successor trustee, should something happen to the first one);

- describe the trustee's powers, as broadly or narrowly as you wish;

- name beneficiaries and the conditions under which they may receive income or assets; and

- set a date or circumstance at which the trust will end.

...you put things in...

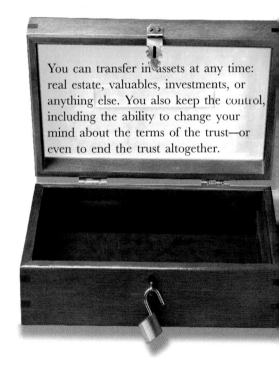

You can transfer in assets at any time: real estate, valuables, investments, or anything else. You also keep the control, including the ability to change your mind about the terms of the trust—or even to end the trust altogether.

Three main kinds of trusts

Revocable trust. You set it up while you're alive, although you don't have to fund it until your death.

Testamentary trust. This is created in your will. It's not funded until the will goes through probate and all other financial and legal matters are completed.

Irrevocable trust. You give up ownership, control, and use of the assets. Irrevocability takes them out of your estate and offers more tax benefits. These trusts may make sense if you own assets that total more than $600,000 (and therefore will face estate taxes). Certain trusts for children, insurance trusts, and charitable trusts must be created as irrevocable to work.

Reasons for a revocable trust

Manage finances. It helps to manage your assets in the best interests of beneficiaries, or to consolidate assets under one legal jurisdiction.

Self-protection. If you become incapacitated, you have a vehicle in place to manage investments and provide income.

Avoid probate. Assets in trust avoid the costs and delays of probate.

Continue control. You can direct the use of your assets once you die.

Reasons for an irrevocable trust

Save taxes. It can help minimize the amount of assets that can be taxed in your estate.

Protect assets. In some states, assets aren't reachable by the beneficiary's creditors, as long as you don't place them in a trust for that purpose.

Protect from divorce disputes. You can usually make assets available to a child but inaccessible to the child's spouse.

...you take things **out**...

You can withdraw assets or income at any time. You're taxed on all the income earned by the trust. In other words, it "flows through" to you.

...and then it **locks.**

Upon your death, the trust becomes irrevocable: the terms can't be changed. Any instructions you wanted to become effective upon your death are carried out.

The trust agreement can be drafted with flexible terms. For example, you can instruct the trustee to make distributions for the "comfort, support, medical care, and education" of your spouse and children. You don't need to list the actual expenses the trustee is permitted to pay.

Irrevocable trusts file their own tax returns and have their own tax brackets. So undistributed income now becomes taxable to the trust. The tax rates, however, are much higher than for individuals.

The basic tax plan

The most basic part of a plan is to properly combine the marital deduction and the unified credit, so that you don't over-use the former and under-use the latter. Property given to a spouse passes free from gift and estate taxes (the marital deduction), which is why many people give their spouses everything when they die. But every person also has a lifetime $600,000 exemption (called the "unified credit"), so if you leave everything to your spouse, you'll forfeit the opportunity to shelter some assets from taxes—and that could eventually mean less money for children. Certain trusts can lessen the tax burden and still provide a spouse with the benefit of those assets. In short,

a little planning goes a long way.

Own assets properly

If you own all your assets jointly with your spouse, everything will go automatically to the survivor. So, if you don't want to lose the opportunity for both spouses to shelter up to $600,000 from estate taxes, you'll need to split your assets so that each of you owns assets in your own name. (If the recipient isn't a U.S. citizen, the rules are different.)

Leave it all to your spouse

It's simple. Assume you have $800,000 in assets. You leave it all to your surviving spouse, and all of it is sheltered from taxes by the marital deduction.

(Assume, for simplicity, that the same amount of money is there when your spouse dies.) Your spouse has a $600,000 exemption (the unified credit), so assets totalling $600,000 are transferred to your children tax-free.

That still leaves $200,000 of assets subject to estate tax at 39%.

The end result:
- $75,000 to taxes.
- $725,000 to your children.

Some useful trusts

Marital trusts. Assets in excess of $600,000 go in here. The spouse gets all the income and, if needed, the assets themselves. There's no immediate tax, but when the spouse dies, the trust is included in the estate and is taxed. With a General Marital Trust, you give your spouse ultimate control over the assets. With a QTIP (Qualified Terminable Interest Property) Marital Trust, you decide who will ultimately receive the assets when your spouse dies.

Family trust. This trust receives up to $600,000. Here too, your spouse may get all the income and, if needed, use of the assets. But there's an added benefit. There's no estate tax upon your death or upon your spouse's death. Everything in the trust passes to the next beneficiaries (e.g., children) estate tax-free.

Create proper vehicles

You could give your spouse all of your assets without an immediate tax consequence. But when your spouse dies, everything will be taxed as part of his or her estate. By leaving your money to a trust designed to take advantage of the $600,000 exemption, called a "family trust," you'll preserve the tax benefits and the benefits for your spouse.

Leave it in a trust

Start with the same $800,000 in assets.

Upon your death, a family trust receives $600,000. The other $200,000 goes directly to your spouse (or into a marital trust). The spouse can receive all the income from the family trusts.

(Assume, here too, that the same amount of money remains when your spouse dies.) Your $600,000 is already out of the estate.

When your spouse dies, the full $200,000 goes to your children tax-free (since up to $600,000 of your spouse's assets can also be transferred out of his or her estate without being taxed).

The end result:
- Nothing to taxes.
- All $800,000 to your children.

Giving gifts

The easiest and most cost-effective way to minimize estate taxes and provide for those you care about is to give a gift. You can give cash, but giving securities, real estate, or even a share of a business can offer additional benefits. In other words,

some gifts are better than others.

Reasons for giving

Transfer assets out of your estate. This will reduce what could be taxed upon your death.

Shift income. You can lower your family's overall tax burden by giving income-producing assets to family members in lower tax brackets.

Shift appreciation. You can give assets you expect to grow in value. This lets you give a small gift without any gift tax that may grow more valuable once the recipient owns it.

Money management. You can help others learn to manage property by instilling a sense of ownership.

Control. By making a gift while you're alive (such as an heirloom or family home), you know that the right person has received it.

Tax deductions. Gifts to charity are usually tax deductible.

What to give

Cash. It's clean, quick, and instantly useful.

Assets expected to gain value. If you give $10,000 worth of stock, for example, you'll pay no gift tax. The recipient simply holds the stock while it (hopefully) grows, and pay no tax on any profit until the stock is sold.

Non-productive assets. Property of value that won't affect your income or cash flow (such as life insurance, land, and other non-income-producing assets).

Low-profit gifts. When a recipient sells an asset that was a gift, the capital gains tax is based on what *you* paid for it. However, if you keep the asset until you die, that gain goes away. The recipient may then sell the asset and pay a capital gains tax based on the value of the asset at the time of your death.

Personal items. Items with emotional appeal, even if they have little monetary value.

The right gift for the right person. Whoever gets your gift also gets your capital gains tax liability once the asset is sold. Therefore, many experts suggest giving assets with the largest taxable gain to people in low tax brackets; and assets with smaller gains to people in higher brackets.

Annual gifts

Each year, you can give gifts valued at up to $10,000 to as many people as you want without incurring a gift tax. The recipient doesn't pay tax on it. (And you *can't* deduct the amount on your taxes.)

For example, you and your spouse could each give $10,000 a year to each of your children and grandchildren, and even to some friends. (One spouse is allowed to give $20,000 and the IRS will treat it as though it came from both spouses, if you file Form 709A.)

Generation-skipping gifts

The IRS charges an extra transfer tax (55%), called the "generation-skipping tax," on gifts to grandchildren and some others. If you have enough assets, you can use a $1 million generation-skipping tax exemption either while you're alive or upon your death. For example, you could set up a trust for your grandchild and fund it with up to $1 million. The first $600,000 would use up your lifetime gift tax exemption, and the next $400,000 would be subject to gift tax. The entire amount, though, would be exempt from the 55% tax.

Lifetime gifts

You can also take advantage of a lifetime $600,000 exemption to make gifts beyond the annual $10,000. Many people wait to use this exemption upon their death; they don't realize any or all of it can be used to make tax-free gifts while they're alive.

Tuition and medical expenses

You can also pay anyone's medical expenses and tuition, without limit, and pay no gift tax. For example, you could pay all of a friend's health insurance premiums and bills. You must, however, pay the provider of the service directly—not the person receiving the gift. (This exemption doesn't apply to room and board or books.)

Gifts after sale. If you give away an asset that has a loss, you won't be able to take it on your tax return. If you sell the asset first, then give away the money, you may be able to take a loss on your return.

No tax if a spouse. There's no gift tax on money you give to your spouse (if a U.S. citizen), no matter how much.

Giving gifts to children

There are many ways to save money for a child's future besides simply opening a bank or brokerage account. Some plans have been created to fill specific needs. Others fill more general needs. All of them, however, like the few described here, are designed

to provide both **guidance** and **support.**

For easy, inexpensive transfers

The Uniform Gifts to Minors Act (UGMA) account holds financial assets. The Uniform Transfers to Minors Act (UTMA) account can also hold real estate and collectibles. Both let you transfer assets to a custodian (the caretaker of the assets, which can be yourself) for the benefit of a minor (e.g., a child). The gifts are tax-free if the total value isn't over $10,000 a year. These "custodial accounts" cost nothing to set up and involve less paperwork than trusts.

Here's how they work:

- You can keep the child from using the assets until he or she reaches legal age, but you can't take the assets back.
- The custodian can spend or invest in any way that helps the child.
- There can be only one custodian and one beneficiary per account.
- Income from the gift is taxed to the child, not to you (see the "kiddie tax" on the next page).
- The assets will still be considered part of your estate when you die unless you've named someone else to act as custodian.

Assets and income can be used for obvious benefits, such as education, and for less obvious ones, including art or athletic lessons, camp, and even vacations.

For more control

If you're uncomfortable with the limitations of an UGMA or UTMA, there may be other trusts you could set up as alternatives.

You can use an irrevocable trust, and name someone else as trustee to manage and distribute the money according to your wishes until the child reaches an age you select. Until then, the child won't have any control over the money, although the trustee can use it for the child's benefit (e.g., an education).

For special needs

If you leave too large an inheritance, your child could lose social security and other government benefits. That's why some people create a "Special Needs Trust." The trust can be incorporated into your will or living trust. You decide the amount to place in the trust, and name a trustee to manage and distribute the money—but only for "special needs." If money is used for basic needs such as food, clothing, or shelter, the government benefits could be reduced or lost.

Save yourself. Sometimes it's better to save for children in your own nam For example, you may want to retain complete control of the assets.

Parent beware

Here are some things to watch out for with an UGMA or UTMA:

- Once a child reaches legal age (18 or 21, depending on the state), he or she is entitled to spend the money or sell the asset without your permission. You will no longer have any control.

- If you request financial aid, the school will consider the child's assets when making its decision. Since students are expected to contribute more of their savings toward their own education than is required of a parent, the extra money held for your child in an UGMA or UTMA could result in less assistance.

The **"kiddie tax."** In 1996, any child with more than $650 of unearned income (income from investments), or total income of more than $3,900, must file a tax return. After the first tax-free $650, the next $650 of unearned income is taxed at the child's rate; and until a child reaches 14, any unearned income over $1,300 is taxed at the parent's rate. This is one way the IRS keeps adults from transferring too many assets to children simply to avoid income taxes.

Life insurance

You can turn a small gift or bequest into a much larger one through a life insurance policy. The eventual cash payout can be a significant amount, but your survivors could lose a lot of it to taxes when you die. There are ways, however, to avoid estate taxes and use this often-overlooked, simple tool

to put in **small** amounts and **leave a lot** behind.

Reasons to buy

Life insurance can help you meet specific goals.

Create an estate. If you don't have a lot of assets, this is one of the best ways to provide a sum of money for the benefit of your loved ones.

Pay for dying. People often underestimate the cash required to pay all the expenses, such as the funeral, taxes, fees, and debts. The payout can save your family from these burdens.

Replace income. Your family may lose your income once you die. The insurance money can be invested to produce income that could replace some or all of the lost earnings. And the rest can be spent over time to cover major monthly expenses, such as a mortgage.

Avoid "handouts." While a cash gift might be spent immediately, an insurance policy ensures a sum kept safe for future use.

Decide what to buy

What kind to buy? "Whole life" can be expensive but works as an investment as well as a death benefit. It builds a cash value that's tax-deferred. "Term" insurance has no cash value but is less expensive. (There are many other types to suit varying needs.)

Deciding the amount is important and takes careful thought. You must balance what you can afford and what you think the recipients will need. Look at debts, income needs, occasional and regular expenses, and expected future expenses such as school tuitions. It's also a good idea to work with a professional to see how much might be needed to pay estate taxes and other expenses when you die.

Three ways to take it out of your estate

This is the crucial step for people with over $600,000 in assets. It means the payout won't be included in the value of your estate and, therefore, won't be whittled down by taxes.

1. Set up an irrevocable trust and have it buy the insurance.

2. Transfer an existing policy into an irrevocable trust. (You must remain alive for at least three years afterward. Otherwise the insurance will be included in your estate.)

3. Give the annual premium as an annual gift directly to a person who buys the policy on your life and owns it in his or her own name.

Eventually, there's a **payout**

Upon your death, the money goes to one or more beneficiaries. If you have underage children, you may want the insurance proceeds to go into a trust that will be managed for their benefit. If you have a lot of assets and want to save on estate taxes, you may want to transfer the policy to an irrevocable trust. This provides the flexibility to distribute annual income instead of one large payout. Even if you think you don't have a lot of assets, it's important to coordinate the insurance with your overall estate plan—because the eventual payout could push your entire estate over the $600,000 lifetime exemption and trigger estate taxes.

The second-to-die policy. This insures both spouses. The payout comes when the second person dies. The premiums are lower than for a single-life policy, but the total cost may be higher since the premiums must be paid for more years—until the second person dies. These policies are commonly used to help provide the cash needed to pay for settling the estate. Consider having someone else—children, or an irrevocable trust, for example—own the policy. That will take it out of the estate and avoid estate taxes.

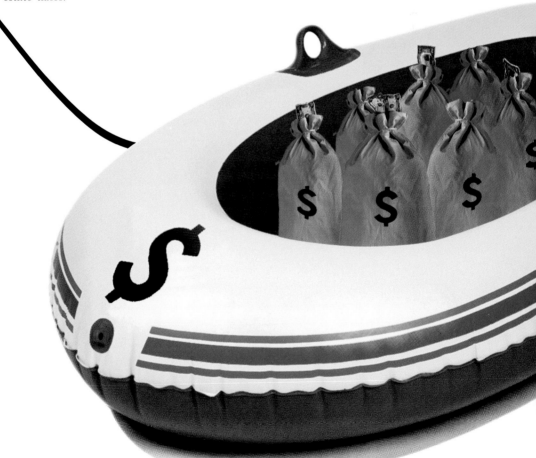

Manage the policy. It's vital that someone pay the premiums on time, monitor the financial stability of the insurer, and follow up on notices and other administrative issues.

Transferring businesses and real estate

Some assets aren't as easy to divide and transfer as others. For example, splitting 100 shares of stock 50-50 between two children is quick and easy. Not so with a family business or real estate. If these assets carry special significance, you may want to find ways to keep them "in the family" after you've gone. One strategy is to transfer ownership

gradually, one piece at a time.

Keep control

There are ways to transfer large assets and avoid the costs, delays, and lack of privacy of probate. One way is to use a tool called a "family limited partnership" to transfer either a business or real estate to family members, and keep control for yourself. You become the general partner (the decision-maker). The others are all limited partners (non-decision-makers).

Give away percentages

Every year, you can give away an ownership interest in the partnership and hold onto the rest. You can give up to the $10,000 annual limit for tax-free gifts to each recipient.

You don't need to go through a rigid accounting process or (for real estate) draw up a new deed each time you transfer some ownership.

Stop when you want

Eventually, you can give away 100% of the asset. You could choose, however, to give away up to 99% of the asset and still keep control of the business decisions through a 1% interest as the general partner of the family limited partnership.

It's out of your estate

Upon your death, most or all of the value of the asset won't be included in your estate because it was transferred to others.

Good strategy for second homes. If your first and second homes are in different states, each home would have to go through probate in its own state. That can be even more costly and time-consuming than normal. Putting the second home in a trust can keep it out of probate.

Transferring home ownership

The simplest way to transfer a home is to add someone's name to the deed. That, however, could lead to problems. For example, if you add a child's name, you would have to include the child in any decisions over the use or sale of the home. That may not be a problem now, but it could be down the road.

One alternative is to place the home in a Qualified Personal Residence Trust (QPRT) and name a child as beneficiary. You give your home at a discount, reduce the size of your estate, and continue to live in the home for a specified number of years. A QPRT is useful for a primary residence or vacation home.

Reasons to transfer

- **Reduce your taxable estate.** Leave less for the IRS upon your death.
- **Shield assets from creditors.** A creditor can't force you to sell the percentage you no longer own. (It's fraudulent, however, to transfer ownership if the purpose is to avoid repaying a creditor.)
- **Shift income.** Move it from parents in higher tax brackets to children or grandchildren in lower brackets.
- **Avoid probate.** There can be high costs, delays, and a lack of privacy.
- **Transfer assets at a discount.** Part-ownership interests aren't easy to sell. That may allow you to discount the value of your gift from 15% to 40%, giving you a chance to make more tax-free transfers. It also lowers the value of the ownership remaining in your estate at your death, which could reduce estate taxes.

{ **Business succession plan.** If you're not ready to give away an asset while you're alive, consider this plan. It involves having a formal agreement that requires surviving owners to buy the other's interest upon death, disability, or retirement.

Giving to charities

Giving to charity, contrary to popular belief, doesn't have to mean depriving you and your children of money. Actually, it may simply mean diverting money away from income and estate taxes—in other words, making a voluntary contribution to your favorite charity instead of an involuntary one to the federal government. Charitable giving, therefore, could be an opportunity

to **tip the scale** and create a win-win situation.

Reasons to give

If you meet the detailed requirements for creating a charitable trust, you can benefit by:

- lowering income taxes by taking a charitable deduction on your tax return;
- receiving regular income while giving away an asset, or giving away income and having the asset returned to you;
- lowering your potential estate tax by reducing the size of your estate;
- last but not least—gaining satisfaction from doing something good for somebody.

Transfer the asset

When you transfer an asset to a charitable trust, you can name yourself, someone else, or the charity as the recipient of the trust's income. You also decide who will ultimately receive the assets when the trust ends.

Create harder-working assets

Since charities are tax-exempt, the trust is also tax-exempt. That means the trustee can sell any asset without facing a capital gains tax on the profit. For example, you may own an asset that would create a large, taxable gain if sold. If you placed it in the trust, the trust could sell it, then reinvest the money in income-generating assets, and not trigger an immediate tax on the sale.

Income from the asset may be paid in one of two ways:

Fixed amount. You designate a fixed amount to be paid each year. This annual payout won't change even if the value of the trust does.

Fixed percentage. You designate a fixed percentage to be paid each year. This payout will rise or fall each year as the value of the assets in the trust fluctuates.

A bonus strategy

Some people actually replace the value of the asset given to charity—plus some. They take the income from the charitable trust and the tax money they saved through the charitable deduction and buy a life insurance policy in an irrevocable trust. The amount they buy usually has a value equal to the value of the asset they placed in the trust. When they die, the beneficiary receives the cash payout—free from income and estate tax—and the charity receives whatever is in the charitable trust.

Keep the income

If you want someone (including yourself) to receive income from the trust, you'll create a "charitable remainder trust." The asset will become the property of the charity, but the income goes to you for your lifetime or a period of years. In the year of the transfer, you'll be able to take a charitable deduction on your tax return based on the value of the charity's future interest.

The trust gets its name from the end result: When the trust ends, whatever remains in it goes to the charity.

Keep the asset

If you don't want to part with an asset, you'll create a "charitable lead trust." The charity gets the income for a period of years. At the end, however, you or anyone else you name receives the asset, and the trust is closed.

rement plan assets

...tirement plan, such as an IRA or 401(k), may be crucial to your future financial ...ay also be a valuable inheritance. Unfortunately, getting money from a plan into the hands of your loved ones isn't always as easy as simply withdrawing it when you need it. The choices you make will affect your retirement income and your estate plan, so it's important to

make the **right moves** and **avoid** the traps.

Three
important decisions

By the time you reach 70$\frac{1}{2}$—the age when you're required to begin withdrawing money—you'll need to make decisions that could have far-reaching effects.

1. How much to withdraw

The IRS sets minimums for annual withdrawals and issues a stiff penalty for anything less. They'll also charge a penalty for annual withdrawals larger than the IRS-prescribed limits. How much you need will guide whether you should take the minimum or more.

Beware! More leaves less

Withdrawals from a retirement plan are subject to income tax and estate tax. So, if your family needs to use plan money to pay for expenses at your death, they'll have to withdraw much more than they'll actually need in order to pay the taxes and still have enough left for the expenses.

> **An alternative retirement plan.** A charitable remainder trust may be better than an IRA, 401(k), or other retirement plan for small business owners or professionals. You can put in more money than the legal limits for annual contributions to retirement plans. There is less paperwork, no plan administration, and no requirement to include employees. What's more, you may be able to take a charitable deduction on your income tax return.

Beware! Conflicts with trusts

If you want to put an IRA or 401(k) in a trust upon your death, be careful. This could trigger immediate tax consequences or a loss of the tax deferral.

2. Choosing the Payment plan

You must choose one of two methods for withdrawing money when you reach age 70½.

Set it for life. You can do the calculation once based on your life expectancy or on your and your spouse's joint life expectancy. You set a minimum annual withdrawal then increase the percentage withdrawn each year. Tables from the IRS show that a 70-year-old can expect to live 16 years, so your minimum would be 1/16th of the assets in the plan in the first year, 1/15th in the second year, and so on, until all the money is withdrawn at age 86.

Keep changing. You recalculate your life expectancy every year based on your new age. This lets you stretch the payouts while you're alive. But it can trigger an accelerated payout at your death.

3. Who gets the money

Who you name as beneficiary will affect when and how the money will be distributed from your plan.

- If it's to go to your spouse upon your death, the money can be "rolled over" (transferred) into another IRA, and the income taxes may be deferred.

- If you expect the money to be used immediately, you might choose someone in a low tax bracket.

- If you name a younger person, you may be able to make the minimum annual withdrawal smaller and last longer by calculating your combined life expectancies.

Settling the estate

Every will must go through probate. It's a public process (so your will is an open book), and it can be costly, time-consuming, and tedious. That's why the fewer assets you leave in your will, the better. Still, probate is required to settle an estate, which means filing your will, obtaining court approval, paying debts and taxes, and

distributing what's left.

Getting started

The person named in your will as the executor:

- files the will with the probate court requesting authority to settle the estate (the person doesn't officially become executor until the court approves, which could take 30 days or more);
- follows the will's instructions;
- if necessary, hires and works with an attorney, a tax professional, and investment people;
- publishes a notice of filing in local classifieds (if no one objects, the court will approve the will and allow the process to continue);
- notifies creditors, banks, brokerages, and others, and opens a bank account for the estate.

Collecting

Locate, collect, and inventory assets. The executor searches safe deposit boxes and other safekeeping places, files for tax refunds and government benefits owed the estate, collects any other money owed, and has all property and valuables appraised.

Review financial records. This includes insurance polices, employment contracts, bank and brokerage accounts, leases and mortgages, tax returns, and business records.

{ **Where there's no will.** If you don't have a will, your assets are passed along according to the laws of your home state—not necessarily according to your wishes. Typically, a spouse gets at least half the personal and real property, and children and parents get the rest.

Organizing and managing

Administer the estate. The executor examines claims against the estate, defends any lawsuits, and sees that cash is available to pay expenses.

Manage assets. The assets must continue to be managed. This may require running a business, managing real estate, or investing in securities. It may be wise to hire professionals for assistance.

File tax returns. The executor is responsible for preparing and filing final income tax and estate tax returns, and prepares for a possible tax audit. The executor can also do after-death planning (including making choices that will save income and estate taxes).

{ **No will.** About 66% of Americans die without a will. About 9% of wills are declared invalid.

Distributing

Distribute the assets. The executor makes any required payments, and then distributes the remaining assets according to the will.

The executor receives releases from the beneficiaries, and does a final accounting of the assets, income, and distributions.

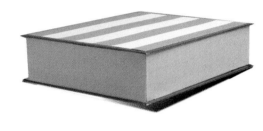

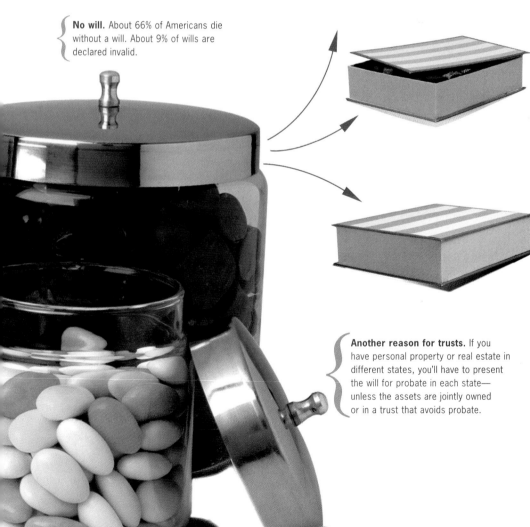

{ **Another reason for trusts.** If you have personal property or real estate in different states, you'll have to present the will for probate in each state— unless the assets are jointly owned or in a trust that avoids probate.

Choosing the people to handle your plans

These may be the most important decisions you'll make. Your choices of executor and trustees could affect your family for years. Should you choose family members, friends, or professionals? Who should be the alternates, in case your first choice can't do it? Just remember, this isn't an honor you're bestowing, this

is a business decision, not an emotional one.

Legal criteria
They vary by state but executors and trustees must be:
- at least 18 (unless married or court-approved);
- not incompetent or incapacitated;
- not a convicted felon;
- found suitable by the court.

Personal criteria
Consider naming someone who has:
Integrity and good judgment. The legal standard is "the reasonableness expected from the average person."
Willingness. Has the person seen the trust agreement and understood the commitment?
Time and patience. Will he or she be able to follow through on all the details?
Organizational skills. There's a lot to handle, sometimes under time and personal pressures.
Accessibility. Will the person be around to talk to family and advisors? Does he or she live nearby?
Familiarity. Can he or she deal with the family dynamics?
Legal and financial awareness. Will he or she understand where professionals may be needed for investment, tax, and legal advice?

A trustee is...

...the manager of the trust and its assets, the one you trust to manage your property. You can limit the trustee's powers or allow full discretion. Some of a trustee's responsibilities include:
- staying within the trust's rules and spirit;
- making investment decisions;
- distributing assets and/or income;
- filing the trust's tax returns;
- hiring professional assistance when necessary.

Higher standards. Professionals acting as executors or trustees are usually held to a higher standard of conduct than family members or friends.

To name an "insider" or "outsider"?

Here are some factors to consider when choosing between a family member or friend and a profes[sional].
(Naming one of each could be a good blend of personal touch and expertise.)

Family or friend	Professional
• May serve for free	• Hourly or percentage fee
• Serves with care for family needs and personalities	• More experienced and efficient; better resources
• Familiar with your business	• Tend to be better at important details
• Better able to substitute for your judgment	• Less potential for family strife, favoritism, jealousies
	• Well-equipped to handle accounting, filings, record-keeping, distributions
	• Investment, tax, and legal expertise

A guardian is...

...the person who will become the legal protector of your underage children should you be unable to care for them. Choose someone you trust and who understands what *you* think is best for your children. A guardianship remains in force until children turn legal age in that state.

An executor is...

...the person, named in the will, who's responsible for settling your affairs after you're gone. That means trying to follow both the letter and spirit of the instructions in the will. It also means handling the tasks of settling the estate.

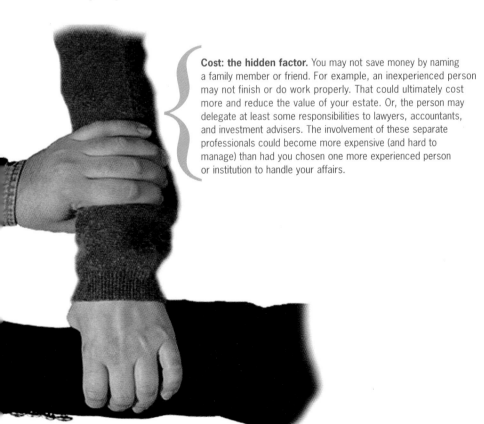

Cost: the hidden factor. You may not save money by naming a family member or friend. For example, an inexperienced person may not finish or do work properly. That could ultimately cost more and reduce the value of your estate. Or, the person may delegate at least some responsibilities to lawyers, accountants, and investment advisers. The involvement of these separate professionals could become more expensive (and hard to manage) than had you chosen one more experienced person or institution to handle your affairs.

Who's who

Trust company
A trust company provides access to all the people and resources needed to manage assets and carry out an estate plan. The company usually assigns a lead account person (the trust officer) to learn about your needs and see that all appropriate tasks are completed to your satisfaction.

Trust officer
The member of a bank or trust company who manages your account for your benefit while you're alive, and for your survivors once you've gone. The trust officer works closely with the legal, tax, investment and other departments to coordinate all the elements of an estate plan.

Accountant
This may be the person who has done the family taxes for years and is most familiar with the estate. The accountant should be able to clearly list your assets, liabilities, and any income due you—the basics you'll need to begin an estate plan. The accountant will also help resolve any complex tax issues that arise.

Conservator
The court-appointed person who handles the affairs of an incapacitated person.

Administrator
The court-appointed person who handles the administration of an estate when there is no executor named in a will.

Attorney
This is the person who puts together the estate plan, sorting through all of the information provided by you and any other advisors. He or she does legal and tax research, provides legal advice, and most important of all, writes the legal documents. This person should understand tax and trust law and be able to apply its potential consequences and limitations to your particular circumstances. The more complicated your situation, the more you'll need an estate planning specialist.

Successors
You'll name people to handle various aspects of your affairs for you. But one or more of these people could, for example, become ill, die, move away, or face pressure from personal problems. That's why it's crucial to have a "successor provision" in which you name at least one or two alternates for the executor, trustees, and especially the guardians of your children. If you don't take care of this, the probate court will handle it.

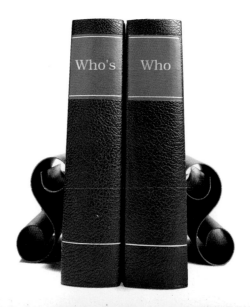

[Appendix]-------->

ASSET INVENTORY

If you've left your affairs in order when you die, you will have helped your loved ones manage the logistics of a difficult situation. This checklist can help you communicate where your assets can be found and how much you have.

Checking accounts/Savings accounts
List all:
- Bank names and addresses
- Account numbers
- Helpful details (e.g., contacts, location of statements and checkbooks)

Investments
List all:
- Institution names and addresses
- Account numbers
- Helpful details (e.g., contacts, location of statements)

Insurance
List all:
- Institution names and addresses
- Account numbers
- Helpful details (e.g., contacts, location of statements)

Credit cards
List all:
- Institution names and addresses
- Account numbers
- Helpful details (e.g., location of statements)

Mortgage/Other loans
List the:
- Institution's name and addresses
- Account number
- Basic terms
- Location of documents (e.g., closing documents, payment statements)
- Description/location of property (if it's not obvious)

Other income
- Social Security
- Other government benefits
- Pension
- IRAs/Keoghs/401(k)

Safe deposit box
- Location
- Contents
- Location of key and necessary documents for access

DOCUMENT INVENTORY

It will be useful for your survivors to know the whereabouts of relevant documents and the professionals who handle your affairs.

Will

Where kept: _____

Executor: _____

Address: _____

Phone: _____

Trust documents

Name of trust: _____

Where kept: _____

Trustee: _____

Address: _____

Phone: _____

Power of Attorney

Where kept: _____

Person named: _____

Address: _____

Phone: _____

Living Will

Where kept: _____

Person named: _____

Address: _____

Phone _____

Healthcare Power of Attorney

Where kept: _____

Person named: _____

Phone: _____

Location of other documents

Birth Certificate: _____

Marriage Certificate: _____

Papers: _____

Others (Deeds/Titles to property/Citizenship): _____

Person in charge of collecting these documents

Name: _____

Address: _____

Phone: _____

PERSONAL MESSAGES

You may want to leave specific messages for people. Place them in separate envelopes and note their location.

Name: _____

Location of message: _____

Name: _____

Location of message: _____

Name: _____

Location of message: _____

Name: _____

Location of message: _____

Other intentions

Most of your wishes regarding your property, pets, or hobbies can be addressed in your will, but you may want show your intentions by making a list of the smaller, personal items. (A photo of the item would avoid confusion.)

I would like _____

to have _____

_____

_____

I would like _____

to have _____

_____

_____

I would like _____

to have _____

_____

_____

I would like _____

to have _____

_____

_____

Pet information

Name of veterinarian: _____

Address: _____

Phone: _____

FUNERAL ARRANGEMENTS

You will have more of a "presence'" at your own funeral if you discuss your preferences with your survivors before the fact. Here is a list of considerations.

Existing arrangements

The following details are already in place:

_____

_____

_____

_____

_____

_____

_____

_____

Requests

I would like to be _____buried _____cremated

Use this funeral home/crematory

Name:

Address:

Phone:

Other details:

Conduct service at:

Who will preside:

To be sung:

To be read:

Pallbearers:

Donations to:

Complete any of the following lines that are relevant to your situation, and add any other entries you consider necessary.

Location of keys (e.g., second home, office)

_____

_____

_____

Passwords

Computer: _____

Internet: _____

Digital Diary: _____

ATM card PIN: _____

Credit card PIN: _____

Other: _____

Important contacts

Financial planner: _____

Reason: _____

Address: _____

Phone: _____

Lawyer: _____

Reason: _____

Address: _____

Phone: _____

Accountant: _____

Reason: _____

Address: _____

Phone: _____

Business contact: _____

Reason: _____

Address: _____

Phone: _____